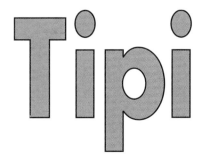

Tipi

Written by
McCrea Adams

Illustrated by
Kimberly L. Dawson Kurnizki

The Rourke Book Company, Inc.
Vero Beach, Florida 32964

Library of Congress Cataloging-in-Publication Data

Adams, McCrea, 1952-
   Tipi / McCrea Adams.
       p. cm. — (Native American homes)
   Includes bibliographical references and index.
   Summary: Describes how the native peoples that lived on the Great Plains built their tipis, the unique dwellings they used for shelter and purposes.
   ISBN 1-55916-275-9
   1. Tipis—Juvenile literature. 2. Indians of North America—Great Plains—Juvenile literature. [1. Tipis. 2. Indians of North America—Great Plains—Dwellings.] I. Title. II. Series.

E78.G73 A35 2000
978.004'97—dc21
                                                          00-025458

Contents

The Great Plains

The Great Plains stretch across North America from Texas in the south to Canada in the north. They reach from the Mississippi River in the east to Colorado, Wyoming, and Montana in the west. The Great Plains are flat grasslands with few trees. The trees grow mostly by rivers. When the Plains Indian tribes first lived there in buffalo-hide tipis, the Plains stretched for thousands of miles with no fences, roads, or cities.

The weather on the Plains is always changing. The summer has comfortable days but also very hot days. Sudden rainstorms or thunderstorms sometimes spring up. In the winter, there are heavy snowfalls and cold days. Strong winds may blow at any time of year.

Until 200 years ago, many kinds of animals roamed freely across the Plains. Thousands of years ago, there were huge woolly mammoths. After they became *extinct*, the largest animals were the buffalo. Other large animals on the Plains included antelope and deer.

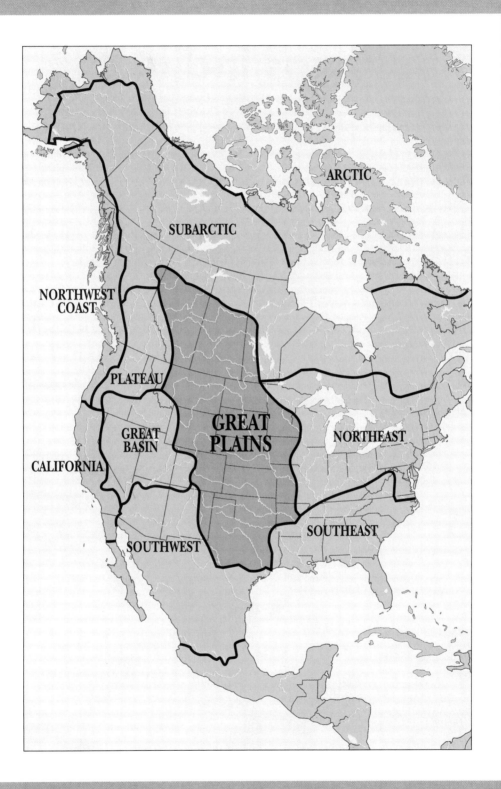

ARCTIC

SUBARCTIC

NORTHWEST
COAST

PLATEAU

GREAT
BASIN

CALIFORNIA

GREAT
PLAINS

NORTHEAST

SOUTHWEST

SOUTHEAST

5

The Plains Indians

Groups of people moved into the Great Plains thousands of years ago. Through the years, these many small groups became tribes such as the Arapaho, Pawnee, Blackfoot, Sioux, and Cheyenne. Around 1800, more than thirty tribes lived on the Plains. They hunted buffalo, antelope, deer, and smaller animals.

Many Plains tribes moved often to follow the buffalo herds. They also traveled to fight their enemies. Until a few hundred years ago, they traveled on foot. Then, about 500 years ago, European explorers brought horses to America. The Plains tribes soon became expert riders.

The Plains people needed a kind of home that could be packed and moved easily. There were few building materials on the Plains, so the Indians turned to the buffalo. Buffalo hide, or skin, became their basic building material. The Plains Indians tied buffalo hides onto a frame of wood poles to create the tipi.

The Parts of a Tipi

A tipi is a cone-shaped frame of wood poles with a cover tied over it. For many years, the Plains people used buffalo hide for the tipi cover. Later, when there were few buffalo left, they used *canvas* cloth.

At the top of the tipi were two big flaps that were sometimes called "ears." These were the smoke flaps. Long poles reached from the flaps to the ground. The poles were used to open and close the flaps.

A tipi might also have an inner lining. This circle of animal skins went around the tipi from the ground up to about 5 feet (1.5 meters). It helped keep out water and drafts. When the winter was very cold, the people in the tipi could fill the space between the outer cover and the lining with hay or brush for extra warmth.

A tipi could quickly be put up and taken down, over and over again.

Making the Tipi Poles

The first step in making a new tipi was finding good wood for the poles. The poles needed to be long and straight. Willow, lodge-pole pine, and cedar trees all made good tipi poles.

First, the men cut about fifteen straight trees. Then they cut off the branches and bark so the surface of the poles was very smooth. If the poles were too rough, they would soon poke holes in the tipi cover.

The poles had to be at least 25 feet (7.5 meters) long for a large tipi that was about 18 to 20 feet (5.5 to 6 meters) across. They were about 2 inches (5 centimeters) thick where they were tied together near the top. At the bottom, the poles were about 3 to 4 inches (7.5 to 10 centimeters) thick.

When the Plains Indians traveled, the poles were dragged on the ground behind horses. For that reason, new poles were needed every one or two years.

Making the Hide Cover

The Plains Indians got new buffalo hides for tipi covers on the buffalo hunt. The buffalo also supplied the Plains people with meat and animal parts to use for clothes, moccasins (shoes), rugs, needles and thread, rope, paint, and glue.

The men hunted and killed the buffalo. Then it was the women's job to make the tipi cover. It took as many as fourteen buffalo hides to make

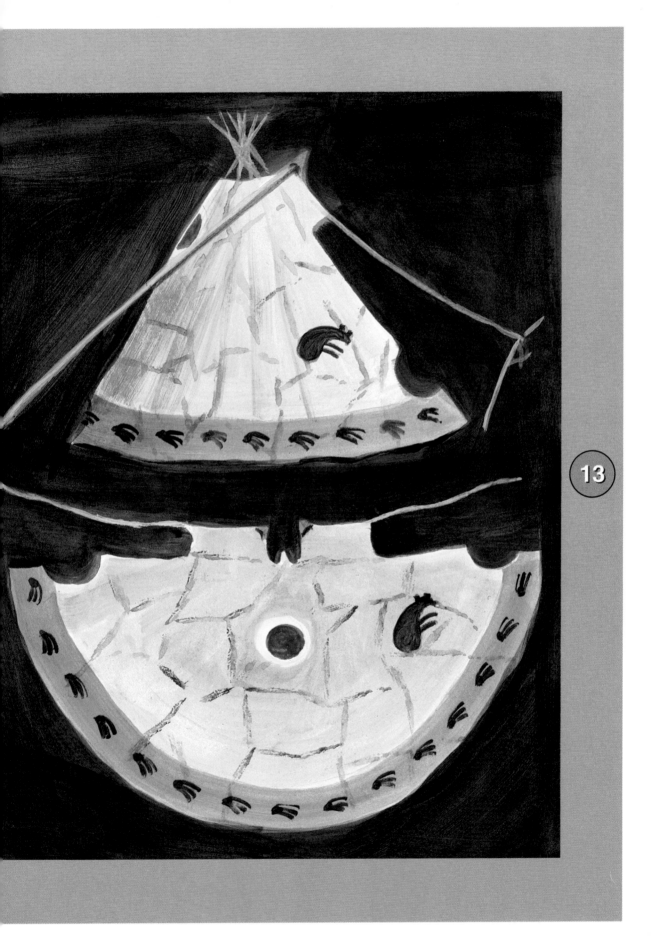

the cover for a good-sized tipi for one family. Once a tipi was made, it was owned by the woman who lived in it.

A group of women who were friends or relatives gathered to prepare the tough hides. All the hard work took many days, so the woman whose tipi was being made gave a feast for her helpers. They scraped and cleaned the insides of the hides, then scraped all the buffalo hair off the outside. If there was water nearby, the women soaked the hides to soften them. They also rubbed them with a softener made from buffalo liver and brains.

Finally the women laid the hides together on the ground in a half-circle shape. At the outside ends of the half circle, they cut two holes along the flat edges to make the entrance of the tipi.

Then they sewed the hides together. They used buffalo *sinew* as thread and sewed with needles and *awls* made from buffalo bone. An experienced older woman guided the others and kept them in a good mood. At the center of the long flat edge, they sewed two smaller pieces of hide to the cover. These were the smoke flaps.

When the women had finished sewing the hides together, they lifted the new cover over the tipi poles for the first time. Then they lit a fire inside the tipi to cure the cover with smoke. They closed the entrance and the smoke flaps tightly so the tipi would hold the smoke inside. Smoking the hides kept the cover from cracking from the weather and helped keep out the rain. Sagebrush might be burned in the fire to give the hides a sweet smell.

Decorating the Tipi

Many tipis were not decorated, but some were painted with designs and symbols. Tipi artists, usually men, painted the tipi cover while it was lying on the ground.

The tipi artist first outlined designs with charcoal, then filled in the shapes with different colors of paint. The colors came from rocks, clay, earth, plants, and animals. Soft red rock and some spring flowers made red colors. Green might come from lake *algae* or duck *dung*.

The artist mixed these colors with a glue made from boiled animal parts to make paint. Then he painted with buffalo-hair brushes, bits of bone, or pieces of softened wood. When white pioneers and soldiers brought store-bought paints west with them, the paints became highly prized trade items.

Putting Up the Tipi

Most tipis housed one family, and the woman who owned the tipi put it up. A tipi is big and impressive, but it could be put together by one person who knew how. The job was easier with

two people working together, however. The women set up their tipis in a circle. Each family's tipi had its own place in the circle.

A woman always put up her family's tipi so the entrance faced east, into the rising sun and away from the west wind. The first step was to put up the tipi's three or four main poles. The woman tied the tops of the poles together while they were still lying on the ground. Then she tilted the poles up together and set them into position.

One at a time, she leaned a ring of thinner poles against the main tied-together poles. A large tipi needed about fifteen poles. Two more thinner poles were also needed to work the smoke flaps once the tipi was put together.

Next, the woman put the cover of buffalo hide over the poles. She tied the cover to the last pole while it was still on the ground. Then she tilted the pole and cover up and leaned them into position on the west side of the tipi frame. She unrolled the cover both ways around the tipi toward the eastern side. Using wood pins, she pinned the two sides together where they met. She climbed up the side of the tipi on a cross-piece of wood like a ladder step to reach the highest pins.

Then she went inside and pushed the poles outward at the bottom so that the hide cover fit tightly. To hold the tipi cover down, she put stones around the bottom or tied it down to wood stakes.

Living in a Tipi

The inside of the tipi was not dark during the daytime, because light came through the buffalo hide. A new hide cover was almost white. As it got older, it darkened a little to a tan or beige color.

A fire for cooking and heat glowed near the center. Only a small fire was needed to keep a well-made tipi warm. Furs or blankets on the ground also helped keep the tipi warm and comfortable.

Sleeping places were arranged around the bottom of the tipi cover. The family slept on animal furs. Firewood, food, and cooking utensils were kept near the entry. The women often baked outside the tipi in small ovens dug out of the ground and heated with coals and hot stones.

For sitting and relaxing at the end of the day, there were backrests made of willow. The head of the family often took the seat across from the entry hole.

Special Tipis and Other Buildings

Almost all tipis were made for families to live in. A few however, had other uses. Plains tribes had special groups such as warrior societies, and these societies often had their own tipis. Tribes also had special large tipis for council meetings.

Many Plains tribes also built homes or structures other than tipis. Some tribes lived in tipis only in summer. In winter they lived in earthlodges. Earthlodges were much bigger than tipis. They were made of dirt and *sod* on a rounded wood frame.

Plains Indians also built large frames to use in the holy Sun Dance ceremony. Sun Dance structures were round wood frames built around a tall cottonwood pole in the center. High overhead, poles stretched from the top of the center pole to the outer frame. Within this frame, the Plains tribes performed the Sun Dance *rituals,* including drumming and chanting.

Plains Indians and Tipis Today

By the 1880's, life on the Great Plains had changed. America was expanding to the west, and roads and railroads crossed the land. Cities were being built. The herds of buffalo were almost all killed by white hunters, and the U.S. government forced the Plains tribes to live on *reservations*.

Today some Plains Indians live in houses on or near reservations. Most reservations are far from big cities, and many Indians living there are poor. Many Indians have moved to cities, looking for education and better jobs.

Tipis are not used as homes today, but they are still important. Some Plains Indians bring canvas tipis with them to Indian events such as pow-wows. They put them up and live in them for a few days. Tipis help set the happy and festive mood for the gathering. At pow-wows, Native Americans enjoy talking and laughing with old friends. There is drumming and dancing, and there is always good food to eat.

Native American boy
getting ready to dance
at a pow-wow in Cody, Wyoming.

Make a Model Tipi

What you will need:

3 or 4 pencils

cloth or paper

scissors

small rubber band

tape and glue

paint, markers, or crayons

To make your tipi:

1. Tie 3 or 4 pencils tightly together with a small rubber band. Tie them about 2" (5 cm.) from the ends without erasers. Spread the eraser ends of the pencils apart and stand them up. Tape down the bottoms so the pencils stay in place.

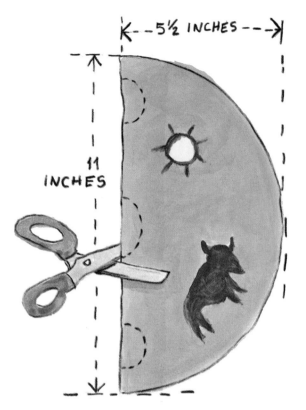

←--5½ INCHES--→

11 INCHES

flat side, about 1" (2.5 cm.) from the curved edge. These make the tipi entrance.

You might paint designs on the cover to decorate your tipi. Paint horses, buffalo, or star designs.

3. Set the cover over the frame. Tape or glue the two ends together where they meet at the entry-hole side.

2. Cut a piece of cloth or paper in a half circle 5 ½" (14 cm.) in diameter. The long flat end of the half circle should be 11" (28 cm.) across. Cut a half circle in the middle of the long side so the cover will fit around the pencils. Then cut two small half-circle holes in the

Glossary

algae: tiny plants that live in water.

awl: a sharp tool for poking small holes in leather or wood.

canvas: a strong cloth of cotton or hemp fiber that was used in tents and sails.

charcoal: the black material left after wood has burned.

dung: animal waste; manure.

extinct: died out; no longer existing.

reservation: a piece of land set aside for use only by Native Americans.

ritual: the form and actions of a ceremony or celebration; often religious in nature.

sinew: tough, stringy fibers that attach an animal's muscle to its bone.

sod: ground or dirt that is covered with grass; turf.

Further Reading

Hunt, Walter Bernard. *The Complete Book of Indian Crafts and Lore*. New York: Golden Press, 1976.

Landau, Elaine. *The Sioux*. New York: Franklin Watts, 1989.

MacFarlan, Allan A. *Living Like Indians: A Treasury of North American Indian Crafts, Games, and Activities*. Mineola, N.Y.: Dover Publications, 1999

Shemie, Bonnie. *Houses of Hide and Earth*. Plattsburgh, N.Y.: Tundra Books, 1991.

Weiss, Harvey. *Shelters: From Tepee to Igloo*. New York: Thomas E. Crowell, 1988.

Wood, Lee Hope. *The Crow Indians*. New York: Chelsea House, 1993.

31

Suggested Web Sites

Native America (native lore; animal totems)
<www2.itexas.net/~sparrow/native.htm>
American Indians and the Natural World
<www.clpgh.org/cmnh/exhibits/north-south-east-west/index.html>
Search Engine Source
<www/yahooligans.com/School_Bell/So...Studies/Cultures/Native_Americans/Tribes>

Index

32

Photo credits: Cover, p. 18, p. 27, Photophile.